Handbook for
Melodeon

by
Roger
Watson

Hal Leonard

Exclusive distributors:
Hal Leonard
7777 West Bluemound Road,
Milwaukee, WI 53213
Email: info@halleonard.com

Hal Leonard Europe Limited
42 Wigmore Street Maryleborne,
London, WIU 2 RY
Email: info@halleonardeurope.com

Hal Leonard Australia Pty. Ltd.
4 Lentara Court Cheltenham,
Victoria, 9132 Australia
Email: info@halleonard.com.au

UK Order No AM 28333
ISBN 0 86001 853 9
© Copyright 1981 Hal Leonard

Cover Design Cleaver Landor
Book Design Cleaver Landor
Photography Andrew Kimm

Printed in EU.

www.halleonard.com

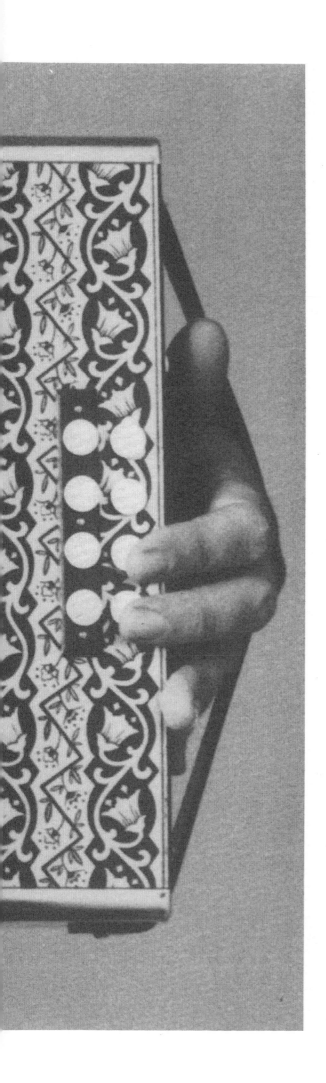

Contents

4   The Melodeon and the Folk Music Revival
6   Diagrams Showing Parts of the Melodeon
7   Diagrams Showing Single Row Instruments
8   How to Play the Melodeon
12 Selection of Folk Tunes
     Winster Gallop
13 Winster Processional
14 Bonny Breast Knot
15 The British Grenadiers
16 Scotland the Brave
17 Brighton Camp (The Girl I Left Behind Me)
18 Dingle Regatta
19 The Rose Tree
20 Strike the Bell (Click Go the Shears)
21 The Boys of Blue Hill
22 Diagrams of Two-Row Melodeons
24 The Two-Row Melodeon: Additional Tunes
     Brighton Camp
25 Constant Billy
     Jockey to the Fair
26 Tralee Gaol
     Jenny Lind
27 Star of the County Down
28 Lillibulero
     Jeannette and Jeannot
29 The Club Melodeon and the Three-Row Melodeon
30 Diagrams of Club Melodeons
31 Diagram of the Three-Row Melodeon
32 Care and Maintenance of the Melodeon

The Melodeon and the Folk Music Revival

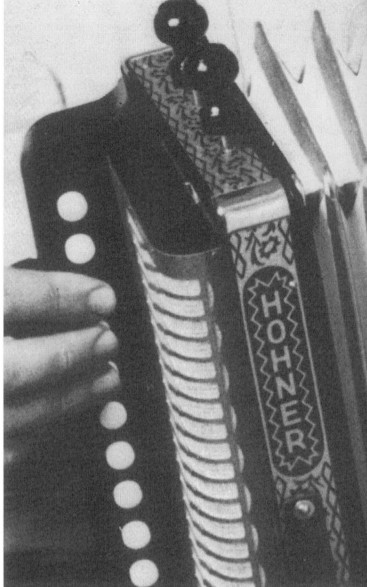

The melodeon is a first cousin, if not a half-brother of the mouth-organ. Indeed, in Germany, the country of its origin, the melodeon is known as the 'Handharmonika'. Christian Buschmann, to whom is credited the invention of the mouth blown instrument, had, as part of his development of the instrument, produced a device with 20 reeds on a brass table powered by a leather bellows. This 'hand-aeoline' was further improved by Demian of Vienna, who first coined the name 'accordion', in 1892. The first serious, efficient and commercial production of diatonic accordions, or melodeons, came from the M. Hohner harmonica factory in Trossingen in the Black Forest, some 50 years later, and it is entirely thanks to this firm that the melodeon ever reached a stage of popularity, in a workable form. The Hohner factory is still the largest producer of melodeons, and offers the widest range of instruments.

The melodeon is also widely used on its own as an accompaniment to Morris, Sword or Clog dancing, where its lightness, strident tone and, again, inherent rhythm make it the ideal instrument to play outdoors with no amplification.

The melodeon is, today, possibly the most frequently used instrument other than the guitar among folk performers. In many areas it has replaced the piano accordion as the basis of dance bands (although the argument over the relative merits of the two still rages), and the melodeon is criticised for its limitations: it only plays in certain keys, and has only a limited accompaniment facility. There are chromatic instruments available, whose two or three rows (usually B/C, C/Csharp, or B/C/Csharp) can be used like the chromatic harmonica to produce the notes of all keys. But the playing technique of these is different, and not covered in this volume.

Whatever you use your melodeon for, the basic playing techniques are not difficult to master, and you will soon have confidence to join in with other musicians at open sessions in clubs or at festivals where new tunes can be learned, and styles and techniques compared. Traditional performers who can be heard on record are Oscar Woods (one-row) and Bob Cann ('Club' system) whose expressiveness and economy of style are an example to us all.

The melodeon is one of the family of 'free-reed' instruments and thus closely related to the concertina, mouth-organ, harmonium and piano accordion. Indeed, it is a kind of accordion itself (and is also known as a button-key accordion): as on the piano-accordion, some of the accompaniment buttons have the facility to play chords. (The German for chord is "Akkorde"). Its origins and early development were in Germany, and it is still to be found in traditional bands in that country, and also in Austria, Italy and other

parts of the European mainland. In Britain, it has always been used as an instrument of folk music, less to accompany songs than to provide music for social or ritual dance. Its system is diatonic in that it plays two notes on most buttons, one when the bellows is pushed together, the other when pulled apart — the same system as the mouth-organ or Anglo-Chromatic concertina — thus giving it an inherent rhythm of its own.

Important note for owners of 'Club' models:
On the inner of the two full rows of your instrument, button 5 (which may have a serrated surface) plays the same note whether the bellows are pushed or pulled. To obtain the equivalent note to '5, pull' where this occurs in the method and tunes, you should change to the outside row, button 7, and pull.

For other detail differences which may be encountered as you progress through the method, please consult the section on the 'Club' model, before panicking!

Diagrams Showing Parts of the Melodeon

The one-row 'stopped' melodeon.

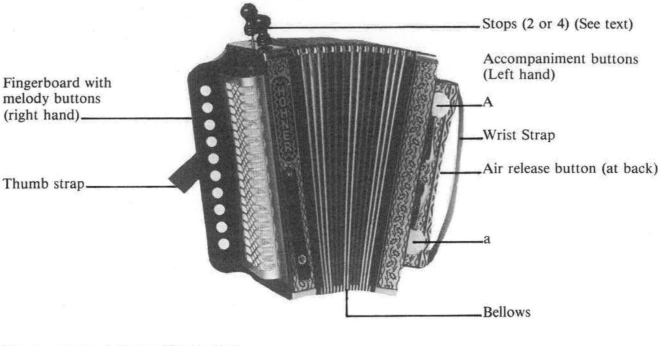

Fingerboard with melody buttons (right hand)

Thumb strap

Stops (2 or 4) (See text)

Accompaniment buttons (Left hand)

A

Wrist Strap

Air release button (at back)

a

Bellows

The one-row melodeon without stops

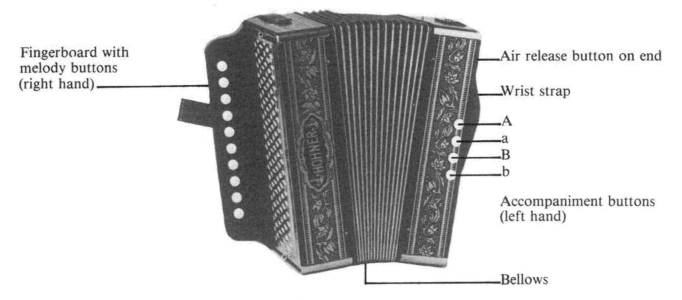

Fingerboard with melody buttons (right hand)

Air release button on end

Wrist strap

A
a
B
b

Accompaniment buttons (left hand)

Bellows

The two-row melodeon, showing accompaniment buttons referred to in text

left-hand end:

Air release button on end

Accompaniment buttons mainly for use with *outside* row of melody buttons

Accompaniment buttons mainly for use with *inside* row of melody buttons

Diagrams Showing Single-Row Instruments

Single Row in C

Single Row in G

Single Row in D

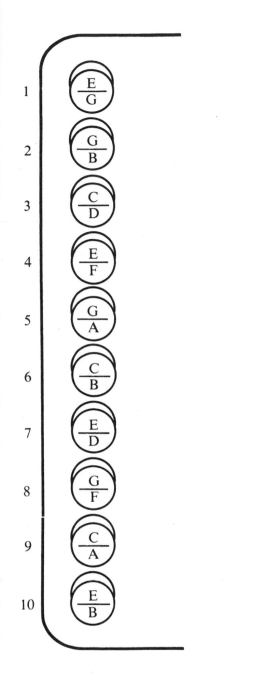

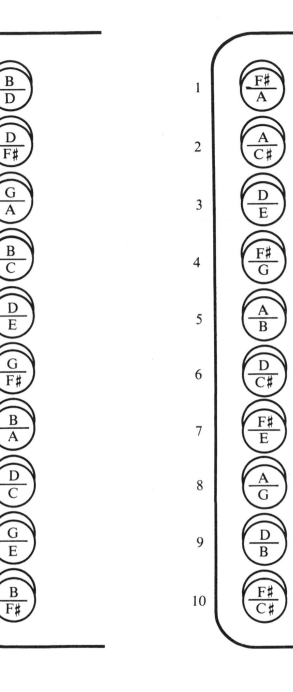

Accompaniment Buttons

a, A: — C Push   G Pull
b, B: — F Push or Pull

Accompaniment Buttons

a, A: — G Push   D Pull
b, B: — C Push or Pull

Accompaniment Buttons

a, A: — D Push   A Pull
b, B: — G Push or Pull

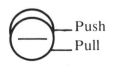
Push
Pull

How to play the Melodeon

The melodeon consists of a set of bellows, mounted between two end pieces, on which buttons are arranged in straight lines. These buttons, through a system of sprung levers, operate pads covering openings in the wooden end, behind which are metal reeds. Thus, when the bellows are opened or closed and the buttons pressed, air can pass over the reeds, making the notes. The principle is the same as for the concertina or piano accordion. The difference is that the buttons on a melodeon are arranged so that the notes for the melody are operated by the buttons controlled by one hand and mounted on a fingerboard. The other hand controls buttons, some of which operate more than one reed, to play an accompaniment consisting of single notes and chords. Most buttons of the melodeon control two different notes, one when the bellows is pulled open, the other when it is pushed closed.

The main object of the exercise is to find which buttons to press, and in which direction to move the bellows, in order to make which notes.

The melody buttons of a melodeon, however many rows there are, are arranged on a finger board protruding from the main body of the instrument. The accompaniment buttons (or levers on many single-row instruments) are on the other end, mounted directly on the body of the instrument. The majority of players hold the instrument so that the melody is played with the right hand and the accompaniment with the left, but there are those who prefer this arrangement reversed. This must be almost impossible with the single-row models with stops mounted on the melody end! The actual holding position of the instrument varies from player to player: some sit, some stand, some hold the instrument close to the body, some brace it against the hip or thigh, but most agree that the fingerboard on which the melody buttons are mounted should be held in one firm position, while the other end is moved to open and close the bellows. To this end, the accompaniment (for the sake of argument, let's say Left Hand) end is provided with a wrist strap, and an air-release button (for opening or closing the bellows without sounding a note) and the melody or Right Hand end has a thumb strap. Many players also attach one or two shoulder straps according to their own preferred playing position.

So, try to find a position which holds the fingerboard as steady as possible, and using the air release button, open and close the bellows a few times to get the feel of the playing position. If the instrument is new, the bellows will probably be very stiff at first. You may find that you have to change your playing position slightly as you begin to play and as the bellows becomes more easy.

Ignore the buttons of the left hand end, except to find a position for your hand which gives you control of the bellows and also leaves your fingers in such a position that they can control the

buttons, and your thumb the air-release. If your melodeon has more than one row, on the right hand end, choose one. The buttons making the lower notes will be at the end closer to your chin, and the further your finger goes away from your chin, the higher the notes. Select the third button from your chin, and after opening the bellows with the aid of the air release button, press this button with your right forefinger and push the bellows towards the closed position. You have played the note with the same name as the key which the instrument (or that row of it) is in. Pull the bellows out again, still fingering the same button and you play the next note up the scale. Now change to the next button and your middle finger, (try it without looking at your fingers) and push again, so giving the next note up. Carry on up the scale by pulling with the same button depressed; then pushing with the third finger on the next button, pull with the same: CARRY ON PULLING with the little finger on the next button, then complete the scale by pushing with the same. So a complete scale can be played using only four buttons. I know scales conjure up horrible memories in many people of school music lessons and the like, but the playing of them does help to familiarise you with the system of the instrument. Anyway, keep trying that sequence, with a smooth bellows action and smooth changes between fingers. Come back down the scale, by reversing the sequence. Try it with a more rhythmic bellows action, and lifting the fingers off between each note. All this gives the basis for the many different stylistic techniques which you will use.

For simplicity, we'll number the buttons on each right hand row starting with the lowest (musically speaking) so the scale you can now play goes: 3 push, 3 pull, 4 push, 4 pull, 5 push, 5 pull, 6 pull, 6 push. Above all, try to do it without looking at your fingers. Now, for the left hand: If you have a one-row, two- or four-stop melodeon, you only have two buttons (or 'spoons') and they play different notes or chords, according to the direction in which the bellows are moved, just like the buttons on the right hand end.

On the one-row model without stops, the upper two correspond to the ones on the stopped melodeon, i.e. they play one note/chord with the bellows pushed, another when pulled. The other two play a different note/chord from those, but they play the same with the bellows going in either direction. On melodeons with more than one row, the lowest two buttons on the row nearest the outside edge of the box are the equivalent to the stopped melodeon ones for the row furthest from the outside edge of the fingerboard. The next two for the row next going out toward the edge, and so on. The buttons on the inside row of the left hand end provide further chords, which will be dealt with later in the sections of this handbook devoted to the appropriate instruments.

Let us then concentrate on the buttons of the stopped one-row, or their equivalent. The use of these bass or accompaniment buttons varies greatly according to style and taste, but one of the most common ways of using them is to provide an accompaniment of bass notes and chords, similar to a piano 'vamp' style. The lower of each pair provides a pair of notes an octave apart, and the upper a fuller chord. The fingers to use for the operation of these are best decided by the individual finding a comfortable position for the hand. Leaving out the right hand buttons for now, try to set up different rhythms with the left, changing direction of the bellows when required. Usually, the single note (octave,) lower button is used for the emphasised on beat, and the chord or upper button for the off beat or beats. Let's call the lower button 'a' and the upper 'A'. A simple 2/4 or polka rhythm can thus be effected by just alternating a & A: a A, a A, a A, etc. For a 4/4 reel rhythm, simply push or pull the bellows a little harder to accentuate each alternate on beat: **a** A a A, **a** A a A, **a** A a A, etc. For a waltz, play an 'a' followed by two 'As': a A A, a A A, a A A, etc. A 6/8 or jig rhythm is achieved by counting '1, 2, 3, 4, 5, 6, and playing 'a' on 1 and 4, and 'A' on 3 and 6 each time.

Now, try playing that scale again, but add a chosen bass pattern. Start with the simplest: a A, a A, etc. and play one right hand note for each full measure of the accompaniment. The secret is to try to get the two hands working independently. Pianists and guitarists will already have considerable experience of this.

Let's play a real tune then! (Thought we'd never get round to it, didn't you?) Try the first one in this section of the book, 'Winster Gallop' Many of you may know it already. The melody can be played entirely on the four buttons already used for the scale. Some players prefer, when learning a new tune to work on the melody until they can play it almost without thinking, (and certainly without looking at their fingers) and then add the accompaniment. Those who have instruments with more than two buttons on the left hand end will notice that the two buttons already used do not harmonize perfectly with some notes of the scale. You may already have experimented with other left hand buttons and found ones which fit better. In the tune 'Winster Gallop' you will notice that buttons 'b' & 'B' are suggested for part of the accompaniment. On a single-row instrument with four bass buttons, these are of course the other two; on a multi-row instrument, they are the ones adjacent to the buttons 'a' & 'A' but on the inside row of the left hand. They are, however, not the equivalent chord for each row, although they do have a similar effect.

The next tune also uses only those four melody buttons. Having tried that, let's explore the rest of the row. Starting with a push on button 6, we can get another scale. Again, start with the forefinger, and play: 6 push; change to middle finger, and play 7 pull, 7 push; change to third finger, and play 8 pull, 8 push; move third finger to button 9, play 9 pull; change to little finger, play 10 pull, back to middle finger, play 9 push. Practise until the change of finger sequence becomes possible without looking, and virtually without thinking.

Very few tunes fit conveniently into one full scale, so most of your playing will span more than one of the already practised scales or parts of both. The actual fingers which you use for particular buttons are a matter for personal preference as is the most convenient place to change sequence when the tune goes beyond the scope of four fingers, but for the tunes in this book, a basic position is suggested for

each of the first 5 tunes. Each time you have perfected one of the tunes in the book, try to think of other tunes in a similar rhythm and range, and work them out, with accompaniments, for yourself. This is the best way of familiarizing yourself with the instrument and of building a varied and original repertoire.

Some players make more use of the air-release button than do others. Circumstances, such as a long sequence of notes with the bellows in one direction may dictate that a 'breath' has to be snatched to prevent the bellows reaching their full extent or contraction. Many players make frequent use of the button to keep the bellows within particular limits of expansion and contraction, and it is true that the control of the smoothness of bellows' action deteriorates particularly when the bellows is at its widest extent.

Stops on Two-and Four-Stop Melodeons

Melodeons without stops have two (or three) sets of reeds tuned at a slight variance with each other, to give strength to the note and a slight tremolo effect. With stopped melodeons, effects can be chosen by pulling out the different stops. With a two-stop model, the stop which is nearest the body controls the reeds in normal tuning, and the other brings in the tremolo reeds. On the four-stop model, the stops in the middle positions are the equivalent of those on the two-stop model, the same pitch but the further one from the body adding tremolo. The very furthest from the body adds a set of reeds one octave higher, and the one nearest adds a set of reeds one octave lower. Obviously, the more banks of reeds that are brought into play, the more air that will be used, and bellows' action may have to be modified to take this into account.

Selection of Folk Tunes

The tunes in this book have been chosen on two grounds. Firstly, they are reasonably well known, and the player is quite likely to have already played them on another instrument, or to have heard them played in folk culbs, at ceilidhs or barn dances, or in musicians' sessions at festivals. Secondly, they each illustrate a different facet of playing technique, explained in the notes for each one. These notes should be read carefully before playing is attempted, and continually referred to during the learning. However, the sooner you can play a tune without referring to the notes or the music and fingering instructions, the closer you will be to the kind of familiarity with the instrument that enables you to learn new material by ear. A possible way of achieving this could be as follows: after each tune is perfected, think of another you know which has a similar rhythm and range, and try to work that out as well for yourself. If you read music, look in one of the English Folk Dance and Song Society

'Community Dance Manuals' or a similar publication for tunes which look similar. You could even write in the button pattern in the style of this book if it helps.

And what if you don't read music? The button pattern is given with each tune above the appropriate note. A number with the symbol ∧ above it, means that the bellows are pulled to make the note, without the symbol, the bellows are pushed. The higher the notes appear up the stave the higher the pitch. The higher the pitch, the further the button will be from your chin.

For convenience, all tunes in this section are written in G. If your instrument is in another key, the button patterns for both melody and accompaniment stay exactly the same. A glance at the appropriate fingering chart will tell you what note you are actually playing.

Winster Gallop

An old favourite, well-known among Barn-dance bands, and frequently played at festival Musicians' Sessions.
Fitting the accompaniment should pose few problems. Note however, that on a couple of

occasions, (namely the third, seventh and fifteenth bars of music), the beat on the accompaniment should come just before the beat in the melody. Practise making the two hands work independently.
Starting position: buttons 3,4,5,6.

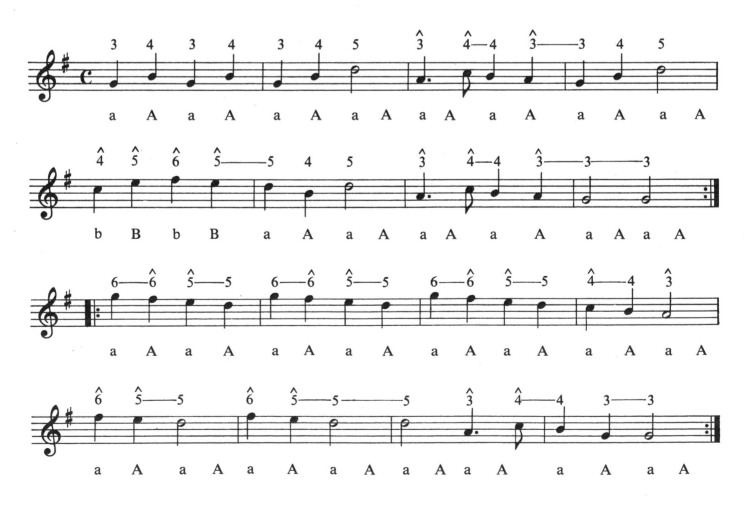

Winster Processional

Like the previous tune, from Winster in Derbyshire. Another very well known tune with many variants, notably 'the Floral Dance'. Also popular as a tune for North-West Morris.

Keep the left hand staccato; i.e. just touch the buttons quickly and fairly lightly; don't dwell on them, and avoid the temptation to follow the measures of the melody too closely. The bars which end in two quavers (notes tied together) have only one beat on the left hand to these two notes on the right.

Starting position: buttons 3,4,5,6.

Bonny Breast Knot

Another popular dance tune.
Uses button no. 2 on a couple of occasions. To adapt fingering for this, you can either keep the basic four button position of the right hand as for the previous two tunes, and use the forefinger for button 2 as well as button 3, or, you could shift all four fingers one button closer to your chin, as button 6 is not used in this tune.
Starting position: buttons 2,3,4,5 or 3,4,5,6.

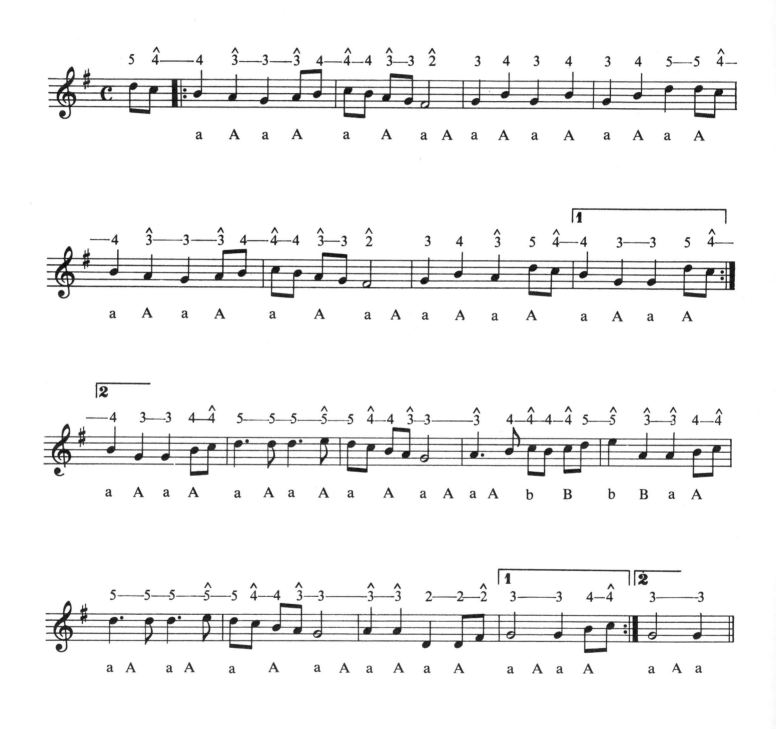

The British Grenadiers

A good march tune, popular among dance bands and North-West Morris sides.

There are quite a few places in this tune where there are more notes to get in on the right hand than on the left.

The tune is played in the upper part of the single-row range and uses five buttons. The first half of the tune can be played with a basic four finger position, with the forefinger on button 5; then, in the eighth bar, having used the middle finger on button 6, move the same finger to button 7 for the next note. Then keep that new position, changing back either for the second half of the eleventh bar, by moving the little finger from 9 to 8, or between the eleventh and twelfth bars, by moving the middle finger back from 7 to 6 again.

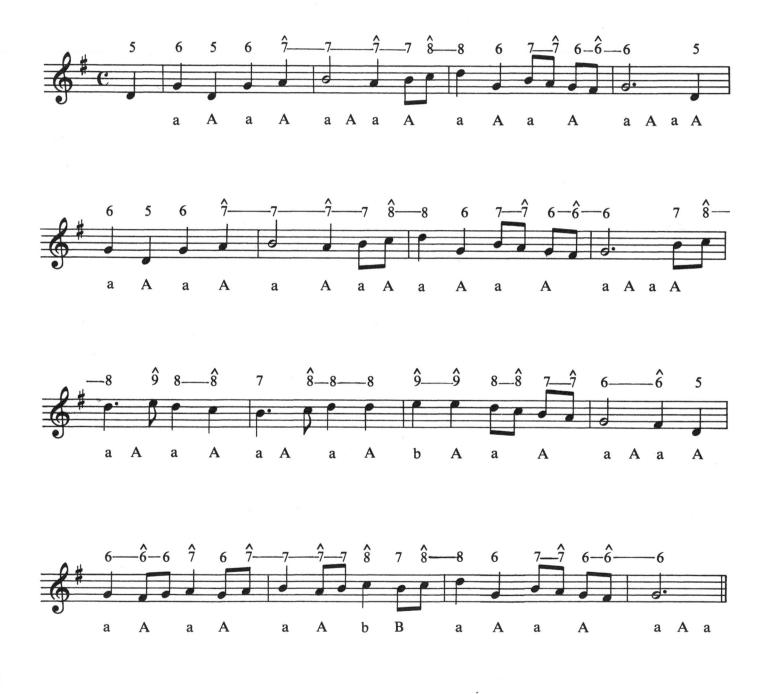

Scotland the Brave

The best known tune for the 'Gay Gordons'. Back to the basic four button position for the right hand, and a jig rhythm on the left. Taking the first proper bar of music, count '1,2,3,4,5,6'. The first note occupies the first '1,2'; the next, '3'; and the other three are '4,5,6'. The left hand 'a' beats come on '1' and '4', the 'A' beats on '3' and '6'. Most of the tune is in the same shape as the left hand pattern. If you have difficulty with the triplets, leave the middle note in each out to start with.

16

Brighton Camp (The Girl I Left Behind Me)

Another country and Morris tune which is frequently heard in sessions.
This takes us to the top of the higher octave on a single-row. Owners of two-row or three-row instruments, see 'Brighton Camp' in the next section.

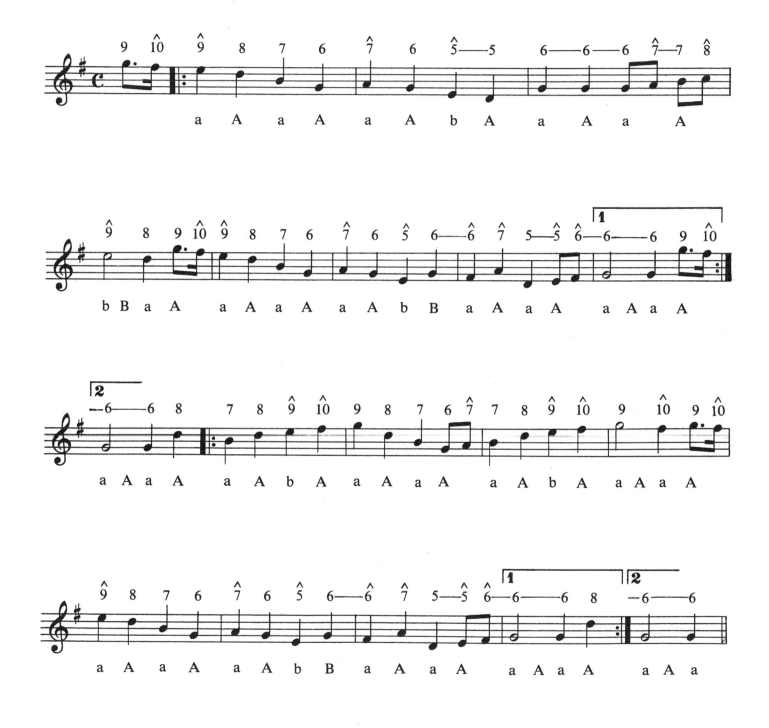

Dingle Regatta

A slightly longer and more difficult Irish jig tune. Great fun to play.

The tune is in three parts, and the middle one uses a higher range than the other two, so you will have to change right hand position again. Try to work it out for yourself this time. On the first and fifth bars of the final part, it can be rather effective to break the normal left hand rhythm and play chords using both buttons together in place of the 'a's, leaving out the 'A's altogether.

18

The Rose Tree

Back to the march, or polka type rhythm, for a country and Morris dance tune.
A six button range to the melody of this one. The position change will have to be made for the first part of the second half of the tune.

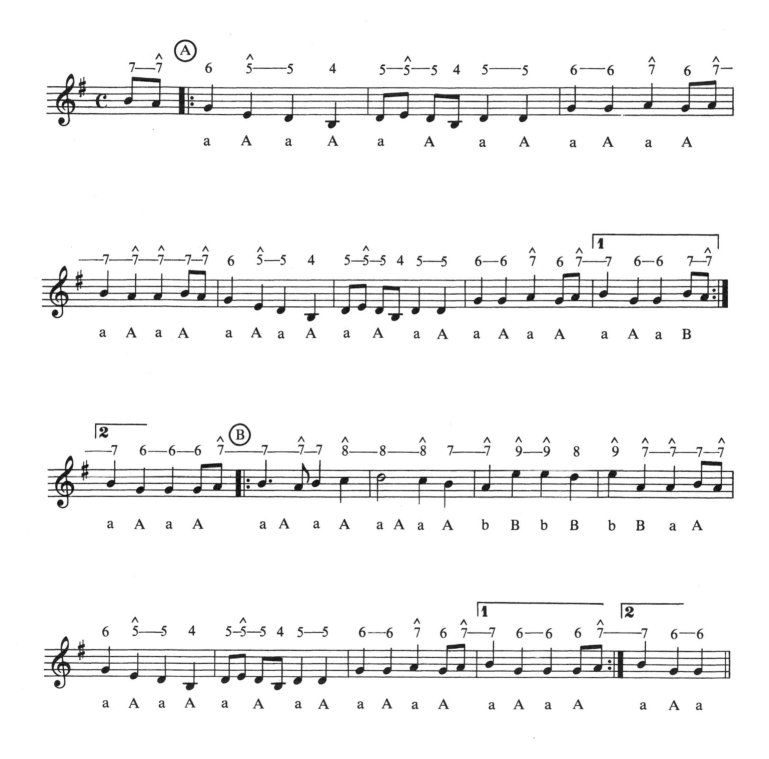

Strike the Bell (Click Go the Shears)

A song tune also used for dances in hornpipe rhythm.

The hornpipe is possibly the most awkward rhythm for the beginner to master, as the left hand is playing much more slowly than the right. Keep the beats of the left hand well spaced out, and notice where they come, in relation to the notes of the right hand.

The Boys of Blue Hill

A hornpipe of Irish origin.
The right hand melody is very full and uses all the buttons from 3 to 9, with frequent changes of position. Work the melody out until all the changes are starting to flow, then add the accompaniment. When you can get this one note perfect each time without looking at your fingers, you are beginning to master the instrument!

Diagrams of Two-Row Melodeons

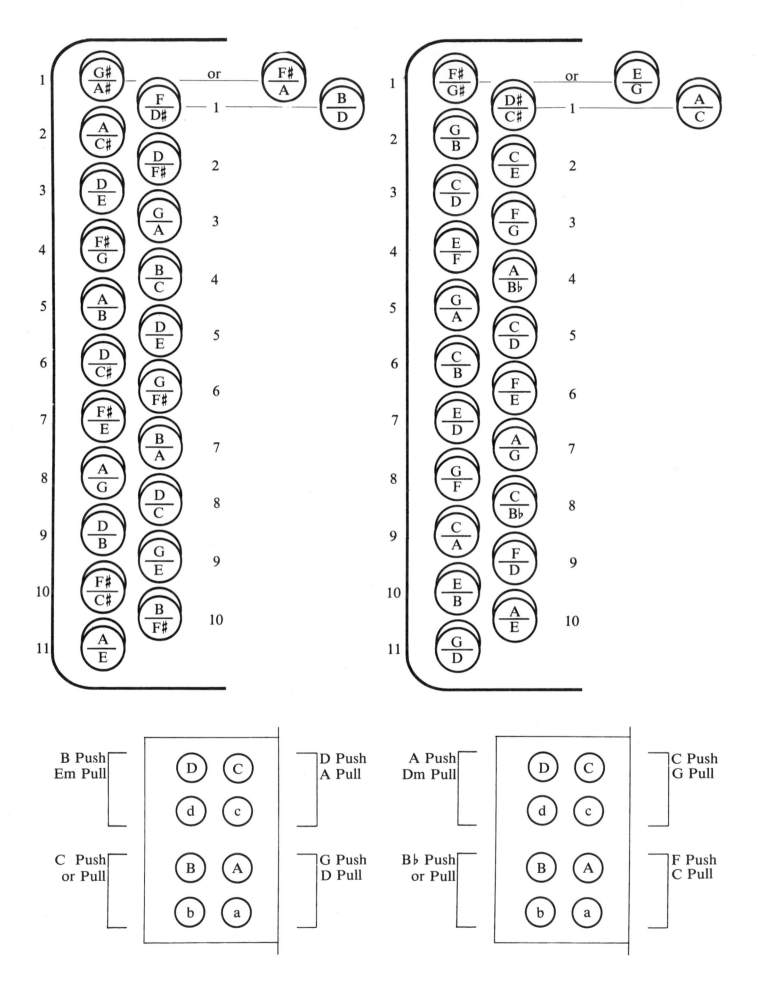

Two-Row in D/G.

Two-Row in C/F.

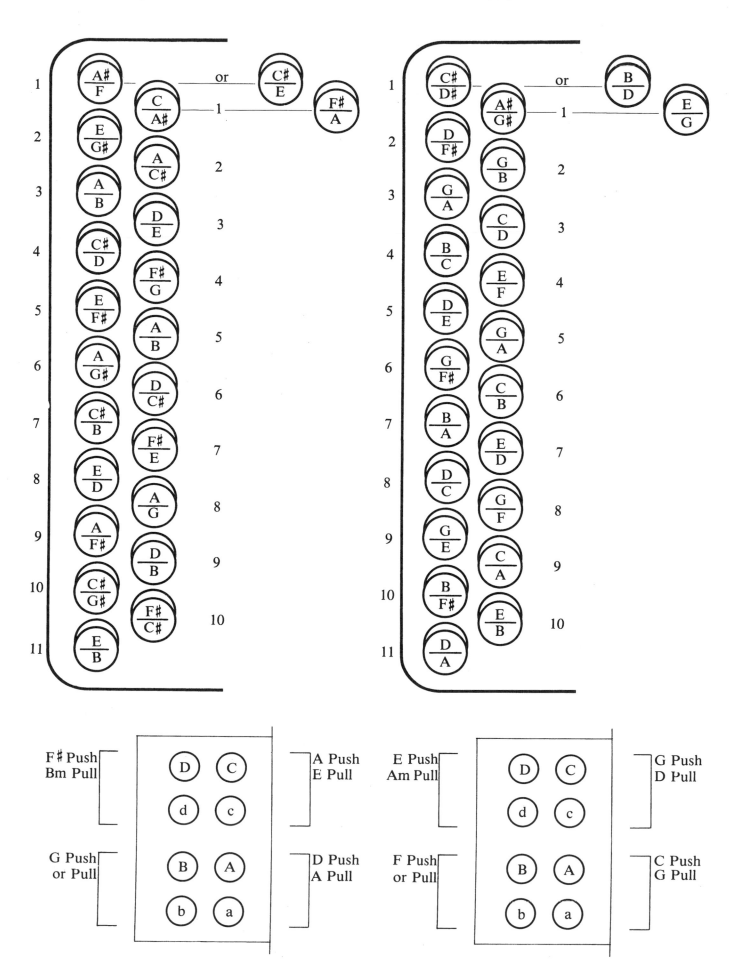

Two-Row in A/D

Two-Row in G/C

The Two-Row Melodeon: Additional Tunes

The first and obvious difference to your playing that you will notice if you have an instrument with more than one row, is that for sheer variety, you will be able to play in more than one key. But the two-row melodeon is far more than just two one-row instruments tied together. By judicious use of both rows at once, a wider variety of tunes can be played, and many can be played far more easily than by using only one row. The scope of the accompaniment buttons is wider, and on some instruments, certain notes which lie outside the normal scales of the instrument's keys are included.

As with the tunes in the previous section, all of which are shown in G, the tunes here are shown as they would be played on a D/G instrument. For those who have instruments in other tunings, the melody and bass button patterns apply just the same.

Brighton Camp

If you have already tried playing these on one row of your melodeon, as outlined in the last section, using the top range, you may have found it excruciatingly high in pitch, particularly on the inside row of a D/G. It is not possible to play them in the lower range on one row; I am sure you will have discovered that the sequence of notes on the buttons 1 & 2 is incomplete; indeed, you may have an instrument on which the no. 1 buttons on each row are tuned to notes which appear to bear no relevance to the others on the instrument at all — more of this later. By using the inside row of your instrument, and in addition, button 3 of the outside row, you can complete the sequence, and play these tunes in the lower range. Use the forefinger for the outside row button. When the symbol * appears in the button pattern, this means 'change row': if you're on the inside row for the note you've just played, change to the outside, or vice versa. The change may only be for one or two notes, so it is as well to keep your hand ready to go back into position to play on the other row again. For this reason it is even more important to keep the fingerboard steady, and at the same time maintain a hand position which gives scope for movement. Really, the only part of the right hand which should be supporting the instrument at all is the thumb.

Constant Billy

A well-known Morris dance tune in jig rhythm.

Jockey to the Fair

A change of rows can also be used to encompass a note which does not exist in the row of the basic melody. This Morris dance tune contains an example of this in the C sharp in the seventh bar. Note however, that the suggestion is that you play the whole phrase on the outside row, thus giving scope for more appropriate chords on buttons 'c' & 'C' of the left hand. The change back is made between the two notes which appear on both rows in the same direction; many other notes which appear on both rows do so on the 'push' direction on one, and the 'pull' direction on the other. If the melody note now exists on the other row in the other direction, you can play the more fitting chords.

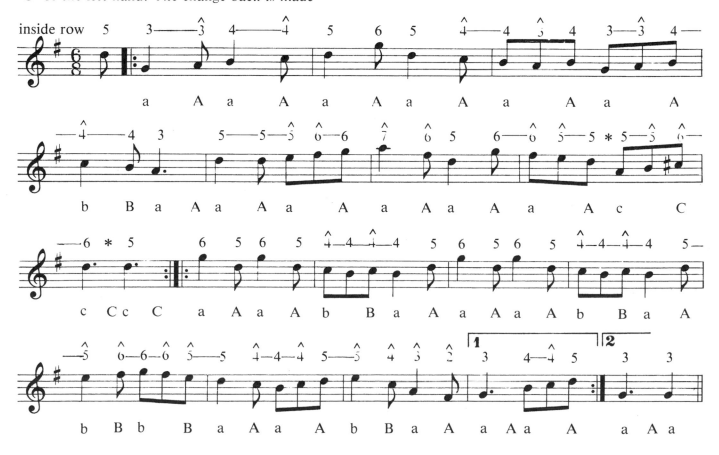

Tralee Gaol

An Irish Polka.

The inclusion of a minor chord, (buttons 'd' & 'D' on the 'pull') allows the two-row instrument to be used for tunes in minor keys or the Dorian Mode. The main difficulty is getting used to most of the important notes of the melody being on the 'pull'.

Note the accompaniment pattern, using the buttons 'c' & 'C' as well. Tralee Gaol is played entirely on the outside row; the melody can also be played on the inside row, but the chords for this are not available.

Jenny Lind

An obvious tune for the two-row instrument, as in this, the most popular of the many current versions, the two parts of the tune are in different keys -

the first entirely on the outside row, and the second entirely on the inside.

Star of the County Down

Shown here as a waltz, but variants of this tune are played in almost every rhythm there is.
Again the tune is basically in a minor key on the outside row, but by changing rows for several phrases, a far more interesting chord sequence can be achieved, using three of the four sets of accompaniment buttons. Also, the whole range of the melody is kept to a fairly limited area of the keyboard.

Lillibulero

A jig or march tune often used for North-West Morris, and as a country dance tune.

This can only be played if you have the 'accidental' notes tuned in on Button 1 of each row, or if you have the 'Club' system instrument. On the ordinary two-row it stays on the inside row even for the 'odd' note on button 1; on the 'Club', it uses one button of the short extra inside row.

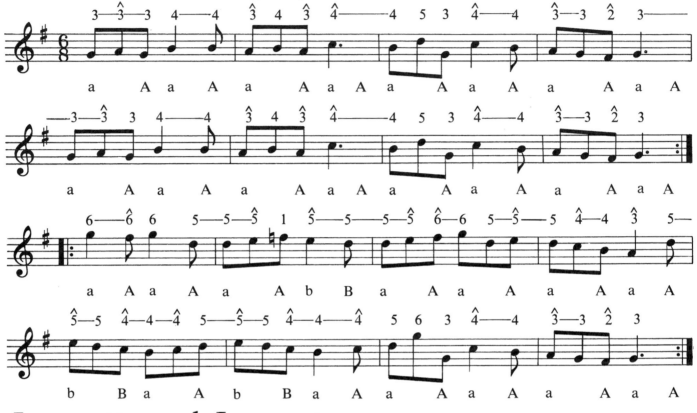

Jeannette and Jeannot

A little gem of a tune from 'France or Sussex' learned from Mel Dean then of the Etchingham Steam Band. I include it as it presents quite a challenge, with lots of change of rows, the use of all eight accompaniment buttons, and the two 'odd' buttons if they are tuned appropriately. Can also be played on the 'Club' with the use of the equivalent buttons from the short row.

The Club Melodeon and the Three-Row Melodeon

The Three-Row Melodeon

The Club model melodeon differs from the standard two-row model in having an extra short row of buttons on the right hand fingerboard, giving a selection of accidentals (notes outside the scales of the instrument's basic keys) similar to, but more in number than the no. 1 buttons on many standard two -row models.

This enables the player to play tunes of a more chromatic nature, and also more modal ones. There is also a button on the inner of the two main rows which plays the same note with the bellows going in either direction. Some older Club models may be found with this button re-tuned to the more normal style.

A Club melodeon may be learned in the same way as any other by using the first two sections of this book. A glance at the tuning chart (plus a little trial and error) will show you where the pattern of the buttons fits in with the standard one. The Club fingerboard, for instance, has an extra button on each major row, nearer to the player's chin. As the

chart shows, this is best considered button no. 0, and then the playing technique as for the two-row instrument (with alternative tuning) can be followed. The equivalent to button 1 in the given tuning of the inside row of the two-row, is button 4 of the short row on the Club; button 1 of the two-row, is button 4 of the short row on the Club; button 1 of the two-row's outside row is button 3 on the Club's short row. The other difference is in the accompaniment buttons; namely that buttons 'b & B' do NOT play the same in both directions.

The Three-Row Melodeon

The Corona model melodeon in A/D/G/ differs little from the two-row models already described. The extra row allows playing in a wider variety of keys, obviously, but also adds an extra pair of accidental notes, and more scope for finding buttons for alternative fingerings when chords or bellows' action make this necessary.

Diagrams of Club Melodeons

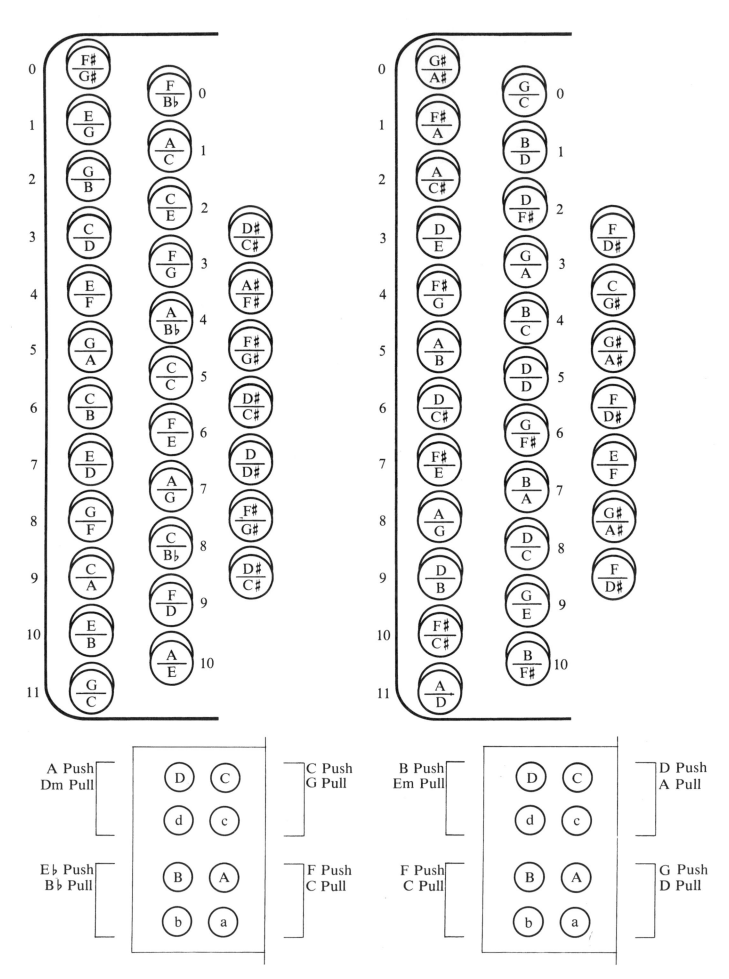

Club Model in C/F

Club Model in D/G

Diagram of the Three Row Melodeon

Three-Row in A/D/G

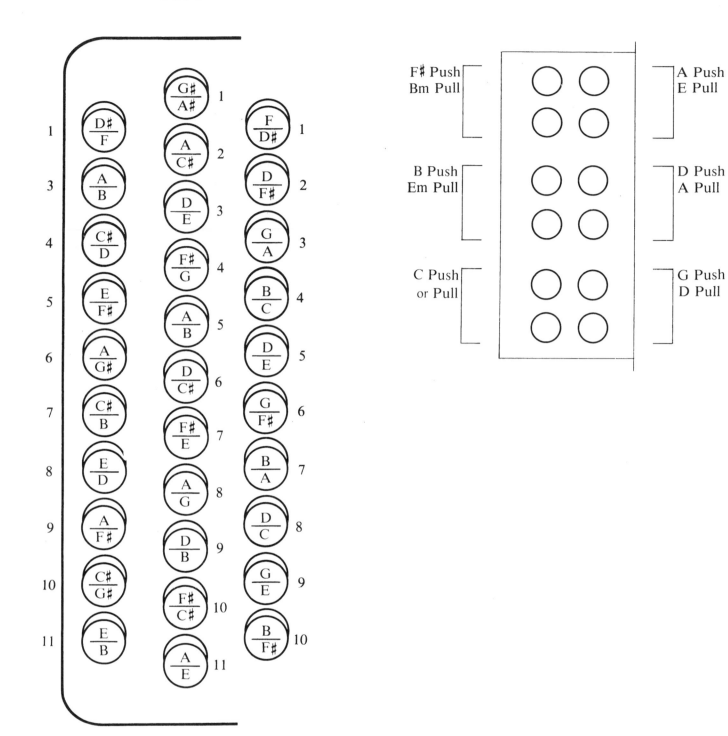

Care and Maintenance of the Melodeon

The melodeon is a fairly hardy instrument and with care in playing and handling should need very little maintenance.

Never open the bellows (or close them) without pressing a button. (If you need to do this to start playing, use the air release button.) Not only would this harm the seams of the bellows, but also enlarge the holes in which the end-mounting pins fit, thus causing air leaks between the bellows and ends.

The reeds in a Hohner melodeon are on individual plates. If a reed should go badly out of tune and need re-tuning or replacement, this should be done by a qualified instrument repairer, or by M. Hohner, Ltd. Your dealer will give you details of the service.

Springs in the lever action may also fail and need replacement from time to time, and this can also be done by M. Hohner, Ltd. There is however, a quick repair of a temporary nature, which can be done in this case:—
Remove the metal front of the right hand end, thus revealing the levers and pads. The unsprung lever can then be re-sprung by winding an elastic band over the lever and round the two adjacent ones. (see illustration)

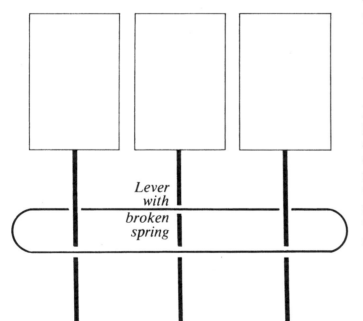

Lever with broken spring

When attaching brackets for shoulder straps, take care not to damage the wooden body of the instrument. If your melodeon does not already have strap brackets, these can be supplied, complete with screws of the correct length, by your dealer, or direct from M. Hohner, Ltd.

If your instrument does not come with a carrying case, cases of the correct size are also available. Some people find an L.P. record case a suitable substitute in the case of a one- or two-row melodeon. The stopped single-row model is particularly vulnerable if carried without a case, as both the stops and the external light metal 'spoons' for the air release and accompaniment buttons are easily damaged.

The Hohner Club Ouverture V Melodeon

Where To Go From Here

Now the real process of becoming a melodeon player begins. Work out your own tunes and song accompaniments by ear or from music. Any book of songs with guitar chords can be used for a start towards working out accompaniments. For dance tunes, the standard collections usually print a melody line only. The more familiar you become with the fingering pattern of the instrument, the easier it will be to work things out by ear.